WEDDING WORDS
TOASTS

WEDDING WORDS

TOASTS

JENNIFER CEGIELSKI

Stewart, Tabori & Chang
New York

Published in 2005 by
Stewart, Tabori & Chang
115 West 18th Street
New York, NY 10011
www.abramsbooks.com

Library of Congress Cataloging-in-Publication Data

Cegielski, Jennifer.
   Wedding words : toasts / Jennifer Cegielski.
      p. cm.
   Includes bibliographical references and index.
   ISBN 1-58479-427-5 (alk. paper)
   1. Wedding toasts. I. Title.

PN6348.W4C44 2005
808.5'1—dc22

                                    2005010901

Editor: Beth Huseman
Designer: Studio Blue, Chicago
Production Manager: Jane Searle

The text of this book was composed in Hoefler Text.

Printed in China

10 9 8 7 6 5 4 3 2 1
First Printing

Stewart, Tabori & Chang is a subsidiary of

LA MARTINIÈRE

For Ann, Kathy, and Adrian
May we someday lift a glass and return the favor

Never forget the days I spent with you.
Continue to be my friend, as you always find me yours.

LUDWIG VAN BEETHOVEN

Through love, through friendship,
a heart lives more than one life.
—ANAÏS NIN

THE CHAMPAGNE CORKS pop and the bubbly is poured—
let the festivities begin! After the solemnity and emo-
tion of a wedding ceremony, the reception is a time for
celebration where everyone can relax and have a good
time. However, in the midst of all the merriment, there
are some meaningful moments. The reception would
be missing something without the heartfelt and humorous toasts proposed by family, friends, and even the
newlyweds themselves.

More than just good wishes for the bride and groom,
wedding toasts are a means of publicly expressing your
feelings for the people you love and a tribute to the
bonds of family and friendship. In addition to the reception, there are many other occasions in the days
and events leading up to the actual wedding that also

call for a touching toast. All of these toasts can show affection, say thanks, and give all those gathered an opportunity to learn something about a couple and their relationship. After a toast has been given, all present raise their glass and take a sip in agreement of what has been said in honor of the recipient.

Toasts through Time

There are many theories on the origins of toasting. One idea dates the practice back to the more malevolent days of ancient Greece, when a dinner host would take the first sip of wine as a good faith gesture to demonstrate the wine wasn't poisoned—truly drinking to his own health and that of his guests. Another possible origin was the habit in sixteenth-century France of putting a crust of bread in the bottom of a goblet to soak up the dregs of the wine, thereby "drinking a toast." Some say, in what amounts to an early version of a drinking game, that a bride and groom would race to drink to a piece of toast at the bottom of the glass, and that whoever won would rule the household.

But from a nuptial perspective, the most intriguing story centers around one legendary toast from the Arthurian era in fifth-century England. During a celebratory feast, a bold Saxon woman by the name of Rowena allegedly raised her cup in honor of the British king, Vortigern, and said, "Lord King, be of health." He became so enamored of her on the spot that they were married that same day.

Early libations included wine, mead, and ale, but modern-day toasters might raise their glasses in thanks to the monk Dom Perignon, who refined the technique for producing champagne in the seventeenth century. It's been the toasting beverage of choice ever since.

Toasting Today

Up until the beginning of the twentieth century, a bride's father generally offered the only toast at a wedding reception. Toasting later evolved to include the best man as part of (and sometimes leading) the proceedings, with a response and toast from the groom. And while women were formerly not included in the ritual, wedding toasting is now open to men and women alike and the custom of several reception toasts in succession is fashionable, with assorted friends and family members joining in when they have something they'd like to say. The content of a toast evolved, too, beyond the simple words "to your health," and may now include anecdotes and jokes, as well as expressions of gratitude and praise. Furthermore, with the modern trend of a multitude of pre-wedding parties, the opportunities to toast have grown.

Regardless of your role in the wedding—bride, groom, maid of honor, best man, mother, father—the very idea of proposing a toast might make you a little anxious. You want your toast to be warm and witty, entertaining and exciting, and most of all memorable. Perhaps you are uneasy speaking in front of a crowd (least of all on a personal and sentimental topic). If you are a bride or groom, you might not have a sense of what it is you would like to say. If you are a friend or loved one who has been asked to share this moment with a newlywed couple, you may feel the added pressure of not wanting to "let down" the bride and groom. While all of these concerns are valid, if you are called to deliver a toast don't worry—it's not as difficult as you may think.

While anyone can give a canned speech, the best wedding toasts come straight from the heart. Therefore, the purpose of this book is not to supply pre-written, generic words for a toaster to simply recite, but instead offer guidelines and suggestions for how to write your own unforgettable and personalized tributes. Cheers!

Love is life.

—LEO TOLSTOY

CHAPTER ONE

ELEMENTS OF A TOAST

IN TRUTH, A TOAST could merely be a little lift of a glass and a few simple words in someone's honor. However, many contemporary wedding toasts have evolved into longer speeches. And while every toast is different in its details, most conform to a basic, logical structure with an introduction, assorted content, and conclusion. Regardless of your writing skills or public speaking abilities, following such a structure will help make your toast feel and sound complete. As you begin to think about your toast now and start conducting your research and commence writing later, remember these three main areas and try to sort your thoughts accordingly. In addition, remember that each wedding toast should have a specific recipient or recipients—the bride, groom, the bride and groom together as a couple, either set of parents and so forth—who are toasted. That is, after all, the point! Be sure you identify the honoree or honorees clearly in your toast. What follows is the general structure of a toast to get you started (see Chapter Four for specific information on writing your toast).

Introduction

The beginning is your chance to make a first impression as it sets the overall tone for the toast, whether humorous or heartrending. Establish whether you are speaking for yourself or on behalf of yourself and others (e.g. the groom for himself and the bride, the best man for all of the groomsmen, father for himself and his wife).

STATE YOUR NAME

At even the most intimate affairs, everyone doesn't always know each other. Unless, of course, you are the bride or groom, make a statement about who you are and what your relationship is to the couple. You might say something like, "For those who do not know me, I am [name], and I am the best man. I have known the groom since we were seven years old at summer camp."

EXPRESS YOUR GRATITUDE

As one of the toast makers, you hold a place of honor among the guests. Let everyone know how glad you are to be a part of the proceedings, and give thanks to the hosts of the event. If you are the host of the event say a few words to welcome everyone.

MAKE NICE

To break the ice or ease your nerves, you can start out with a few pleasantries—something about the appearance of the bride and groom, beauty of the setting, co-operation of the weather—before you get into the real meat of your toast.

Content

At this point, you can take the opportunity to get a little personal and share some of your first hand knowledge about the couple, or, if you are the bride or groom, share a few aspects of your relationship.

Anecdotes provide some insight into a bride and groom's lives, both separately and together, and help explain what brought them to this moment. These stories can include lifetime highlights, reminiscences, humorous recollections, or courtship recaps. The bride and groom might share the story of how they met, the details of their proposal, or some funny stories about the wedding planning. If you are someone toasting the couple together, you can speak about them as individuals first, then as a couple. You might share your first impressions of them, tell what were they like as kids, or recall when they first became an item or how you knew it was love. Everyone always loves to hear theories on why they are a great couple, what is special about their relationship, or other laudatory observations.

OFFER A BIT OF WEDDING ADVICE

Depending on who you are—the parents of the bride who have been married for thirty years, the very-happily-single best man—this advice can be real or tongue-in-cheek. If you have none of your own to offer, you might wish to use a quote (see Chapter Seven) or talk to some long-married couples you know for their often surprising answers.

Or two. Even if your toast has been a humorous one, it's good to end on a sincere note. The bride and groom will undoubtedly have some hopes and dreams for their future to proclaim before their loved ones. If you are toasting the couple, offer some positive reinforcement as you congratulate them as they enter married life. These wishes generally make a nod to themes of love, life, joy, health, prosperity, longevity, serendipity, faith, and overall happiness.

Conclusion

Once you've said all you wish to say, it's time for the actual raising of the glass. If you like, you can end your personal words with a traditional toast ditty (you'll find some examples on pages 108–110), but this isn't mandatory. Simply transition to your conclusion by saying something like, "May I ask you to stand and join me in toasting..." You can also end by saying, "To [name/names]!" and extending your glass in the direction of the toastee before taking a sip.

Variations

While this is the most essential of wedding toast formats, it isn't the only one. If you are looking for something a little different and you are a creative writer, you may choose to set up your toast like a story that builds from the beginning to the end. Carry a theme (fate, everlasting love, opposites attract) or metaphor (love is like a tree) throughout the toast, which you could bring full circle at the close. For a less formal wedding, you might try a novel approach like a top ten list (Top Ten Reasons Why Liz and Ed are Made for Each Other) or a toast set to the rhythm or meter of a well-known song or poem.

Everything comes to us from others.
To be is to belong to someone.
—JEAN-PAUL SARTRE

CHAPTER TWO

THE MAIN EVENT: RECEPTION TOASTS

∾

BEFORE YOU GET STARTED writing your toast, it is helpful to understand your role in the toasting lineup with respect to your position in the wedding. Most people generally associate wedding toasts with those given at the reception (for other appropriate times to toast, see Chapter Three).

Anyone who makes a toast at a wedding reception should have permission from the bride and groom to speak (see Chapter Six for more on etiquette). The couple may specifically ask different people such as their parents, best man, or maid of honor to make a toast. If you are not one of these people and are considering making a toast but haven't formally been asked, be sure to clear things with the bride and groom first.

What follows is a guide according to your role. Outlined below are the points during the reception you would toast, to whom you might direct your toast (while you may open your toast to more than one person, you don't have to include everyone suggested on the list below), and some topics often covered in a toast by someone in your position. Of course, you are free to add recipients and sentiments as you see fit.

The Father/Parents of the Bride

The father of the bride can deliver a toast to his daughter and her new husband by himself or on behalf of himself and his wife, or sometimes the bride's father and mother deliver the toast together. This toast presents an amazing opportunity for parents to tell their daughter how much she means to them and let everyone know how wonderful they think she is. Oftentimes this is the most sentimental of the toasts.

WHEN

As the traditional host of the wedding, the father/parents of the bride reserve the right to propose the first toast. However, while customary, it is not mandatory for the father/parents of the bride to toast. If he/they forgo saying a few words, the best man assumes the role of first toaster.

~~~
WHO
~~~

The father or parents of the bride might raise their glass in honor of:
- The bride
- The newlywed couple
- All the friends and family who have gathered

~~~
TOASTING TOPICS
~~~

As the first toaster, the father/parents of the bride have the honor and distinction of being the first to publicly congratulate the couple. There are many facets to this toast, and the father/parents of the bride might choose to touch on some or all of the following:
- Congratulate his/their daughter and her new husband
- Welcome all the guests to the celebration (if he/they are the host)
- Extend an especially warm welcome to the groom and his family, and comment upon the union of their families
- Thank the wedding party for all their hard work
- Relay touching reminiscences about his/their daughter (the day she was born, growing up, first dates, the

quick passing of time) or recall childhood stories or traits that relate to who she has become

- Tell the story of his/their first meeting with the groom, what it was like to have the groom asking for the bride's hand, what his/their feelings were at the time
- Express his/their feelings about "giving away" his/their daughter to the groom
- Make a statement about how proud he is/they are
- Reveal some funny stories about the wedding planning process
- Offer some words of wisdom or marriage advice; may say something about his/their own marriage and each other
- Thank everyone for sharing in the day, and give special thanks to those who have traveled a long way

The Bride and Groom

The groom can propose his toast solo or on behalf of himself and his bride. The bride may elect to deliver her own independent toast. Alternatively, the groom and bride may wish to make their toast together as one of their first joint activities as newlyweds.

If his newly-minted father-in-law has commenced the toasting, the groom would speak second and offer a response toast with a few words of thanks before continuing with his main toast. The groom often makes a special toast to the bridesmaids for their friendship and for helping his bride prepare for the day (he may choose to delegate this task to best man). The bride could follow the groom, or speak at the end of the series of toasters after the best man and maid of honor. If the father of the bride doesn't toast first, the groom would follow the best man's kick-off toast as the second speaker. Again, the bride could follow the groom's toast, or speak at the end after the best man and maid of honor.

Some of the people the happy couple might direct their toast to:

- Each other
- Any children of their own or those they may already have together
- Their parents/inlaws
- Their grandparents
- Their guests

- The best man, maid of honor, and the wedding party
- Their siblings

TOASTING TOPICS

As the couple of the hour, there is a lot the bride and groom might wish to say. Part of the toast may echo some of the sentiments from their vows, but they may want to split up certain topics between them. For example, one could thank the guests while the other could thank the bridal party to avoid repetition. Whether they toast together or separately, the bride and groom might:

- Compliment their new spouse and give thanks for their partner's love and understanding
- Reveal something about their courtship through a funny or poignant story
- Say how lucky, proud, or happy they feel at becoming a husband or wife
- Declare their love, hopes for the future, and promises to each other
- Acknowledge those whose marriages are an inspiration (grandparents, godparents, etc.)
- Thank their new in-laws for raising such an amazing daughter or son, and let them know how honored they feel to become part of their family

- Thank their own parents for their unconditional love, sacrifices, or generosity
- Thank both sets of parents for giving them their blessing
- Thank the best man, maid of honor, and wedding party for their friendship and support
- Thank guests for sharing in their day and tell them how much their presence means to them
- Thanks to all who helped in the wedding planning process
- Thanks to anyone who may have played a role in bringing the couple together
- Encourage everyone to enjoy themselves during the reception

The Best Man

An essential at every wedding, the best man's toast is often one of the most anticipated. The tone of the toast may be poignant or humorous. In the British tradition, the best man's speech usually includes a jesting character assassination of the groom, complete with assorted props and sometimes audience participation. American toasts oftentimes give the groom a good ribbing, but are somewhat more restrained. The best man should decide what is appropriate for the formality of the occasion and his relationship with the groom.

WHEN

Traditionally the best man's toast would follow the toasts of the father of the bride and the groom. If the groom has proposed a toast to the bridesmaids, the best man can respond to the groom's toast on the bridesmaids' behalf. He may also add some compliments and thanks to them of his own before beginning his toast to the couple. If the bride's father does not toast first, the best man may lead the proceedings, and the groom would follow him.

WHO

The best man may direct his toast to:
• The bride and groom
• The bridesmaids

The best man may focus on a variety of subjects, but his main goal is to toast the bride and groom together. He may say a few words to:

- Compliment the bride and groom
- Say what an honor and a privilege it is to be a part of the wedding
- Offer thanks to the groom (and bride!) for the opportunity to serve as best man
- Reminisce about his friendship with the groom (how they met, notable events throughout their relationship, the qualities he admires in him)
- Recall the first time he met the bride or realized the impact she had on the groom
- Let the bride know how happy she has made the groom
- Comment on how lucky the bride and groom are to have found each other
- Offer praise for their compatibility
- Cheer the couple on as they embrace this new chapter in life together
- Express his congratulations and best wishes

CHILDREN AND TOASTING

With the evolution of the modern family, brides and grooms may gain a lot more than just a new spouse when they are married. One or both parties may have children from a previous relationship, or even children of their own together prior to their marriage. With this in mind and depending on a child's age and feelings on the matter, it is a lovely gesture to include children in the toasting, both as recipients of a toast from their parent/s or new step-parent or as toast makers to the bride and groom themselves.

∼ TOASTS TO CHILDREN

As a bride and groom unite and make a commitment to one another, they also make a commitment to their children and their new family. The parent of a child might stress his or her love for the child and how happy he or she is to be able to share their love together with his or her new spouse. Similarly, someone marrying a person with a child might express joy at becoming a parent to his or her new spouse's child and a commitment to love the child as he or she loves the parent. A couple marrying with existing children might take the opportunity to comment upon how the marriage will strengthen their family and love for one another.

∼ TOASTS FROM CHILDREN

School age children might offer a simple wish or congratulations or thank you to the new member of their family, while teens will have a unique perspective on their new family dynamic and may even joke about a parent's dating and courtship.

The Maid of Honor

A relatively new addition to the proceedings, the maid of honor's toast is not bound by the same conventions as a traditional toast. It does, however, offer an additional point of view on the bride and groom as a couple, and, like the best man's toast, the tone may be humorous or poignant.

WHEN

As this is more of a "bonus" toast, it can be given wherever it fits best. Perhaps the maid of honor could speak directly after the best man or even after the bride and groom.

WHO

The maid of honor may direct her toast to:
• The bride
• The bride and groom
• The ushers and groomsmen

Often utilizing humor, the maid of honor may say a few words to:

- Compliment the bride and offer thanks for being asked to be part of the day
- Tell amusing stories about her relationship with the bride
- Relive moments from the past that convey aspects of the bride's personality
- Share what she thought when she first met the groom
- Reveal when she knew it was love for bride and groom
- Recall what it was like to help during the planning process
- Pay compliments to the ushers on behalf of bridesmaids
- Offer her sincere congratulations and best wishes to the bride and groom

Father/Parents of the Groom

It is not traditional for the parents of the groom to propose a toast at the reception, but by all means find a place for them somewhere in the lineup if they are interested in making a toast.

WHEN

The father or parents of the groom might follow the toast by the groom and his bride as a sort of response to their toast, or they may speak last to conclude the series of toasts.

WHO

The toast may be directed toward:
- The bride and groom
- The bride's parents

TOASTING TOPICS

Some of the same points as in the father/parents of the bride's speech (see pages 11–12) can be touched upon in the groom's parents' toast. In addition, this toast might also contain a few words to:
- describe his/their son's childhood and character
- express happiness about the wedding and joy in gaining a new daughter-in-law
- offer best wishes, congratulations, and hopes for the couple's future

The one thing we can never get enough of is love.
And the one thing we can never give enough of is love.

— HENRY MILLER

CHAPTER THREE

MORE CELEBRATIONS: TOASTS FOR OTHER TIMES

WHILE THE TOASTS at the wedding reception are arguably the most well known and widely given, they are not the only opportunity to say a few words. There are several events leading up to the big day where a toast would be appropriate, even expected, depending on your place in the wedding lineup. In their different incarnations, toasts take on different tones. The formality of the gathering, its purpose and its guest list all have some bearing on the content of a toast. For example, the toast at a bachelor or bachelorette party spent with pals would most likely be considerably spicier than a toast given at a bridal shower where grandmothers or young cousins are in attendance.

The Engagement Party

Traditionally hosted by the bride's parents, this celebration is sometimes hosted by friends or, for a modern twist, by the couple themselves. Engagement parties can be intimate affairs where select friends and family members mix and mingle (sometimes for the very first time), or bustling bashes where everyone knows each other and the guest list is nearly as big as the wedding reception guest list.

FATHER/PARENTS OF THE BRIDE

Essential for any engagement party is a toast from the bride's father to his daughter and to his future son-in-law and his family. While the father traditionally speaks on the mother's behalf, contemporary moms are getting in on the act as well. In addition to the basics below, the toast may also include reminiscences about the bride growing up and any anecdotes regarding the proposal or events leading up to it.

- An announcement of the engagement of the bride and groom
- Thanks to all for attending
- Welcome to groom and his family
- Comments on the joining of their two families
- Congratulations to the happy couple

GROOM

The groom traditionally offers a response to his future father-in-law's toast. He may speak alone or with his bride-to-be to thank the party hosts and guests.

- Thanks to father-in-law for his toast
- Thanks to hosts of party (if the hosts are not future in-laws)
- Thanks to guests in attendance and for any gifts received
- Thanks to his fiancée for saying yes
- His happiness at becoming part of the bride's family
- Anecdotes regarding how and when the proposal happened
- Might also announce potential wedding date

HOSTS

If someone other than the bride's parents host an engagement party, they are welcome to toast the couple.

- Brief explanation of relationship to bride and groom
- Joy at being able to host the event
- Compliments and congratulations to the couple

Anyone from siblings to future wedding party members (if they have already been chosen) may also wish to say a few words.

- Brief explanation of relationship to bride and groom
- Any anecdotes regarding the couple's relationship or their engagement
- Compliments and congratulations to the couple

The Bridal Shower

While a traditional bridal shower is a female affair, many contemporary couples are leveling the playing field and celebrating with "co-ed" showers. The bridal shower toast is one of those where the content varies depending on the guest list—there may be racy references to the upcoming honeymoon during a friends-of-the-bride lingerie shower, more tame observations on women's bonds of family and friendship for a gathering of generations of relatives, or toasts saluting the building of the newlywed nest for showers in mixed company.

HOST

Typically this party is hosted by bridesmaids, friends or relatives who are not immediate family members.

- Welcome and thanks to all for coming
- Wishes for bride and groom as they set up their new home
- Congratulations to the couple

BRIDE

The guest of honor responds to the host's toast and offers up some laudatory words of her own.

- Thanks to host
- Thanks to all in attendance
- Expresses gratitude for the thoughtfulness of all gifts
- Thanks and compliments to bridesmaids for their support during the wedding planning process
- Acknowledgement of special women the bride holds dear—mom, grandmother, godmother, favorite aunt, sister, maid of honor

MAID OF HONOR

This toast could be considered a warm-up for any words the maid of honor plans to say at the reception. If it's a "co-ed" shower, the best man might also speak.

- Thanks to host
- Excitement at being part of the wedding party
- Some good-hearted teasing of bride; funny stories and memories
- What it means to have bride as a friend
- Congratulations to bride

MOM

Since mothers don't traditionally speak at most wedding-related events, the shower presents a good opportunity to say something in an intimate setting to the bride-to-be. Sisters may also propose a toast along similar lines.

- Thanks to host and those who have attended
- How much she loves her daughter and how proud she is
- Her feelings as her daughter starts her own marriage/family/home
- Funny stories about the bride growing up
- Marriage advice
- Congratulations to bride

The Bridesmaids' Luncheon

To thank the bridesmaids and maid of honor for carrying out their duties with aplomb, the bride and/or her mother might arrange for a luncheon or spa afternoon or some similar activity shortly before the wedding takes place. This event may be in lieu of or in addition to a bachelorette party, but either way it is strictly "for the girls." While many of the sentiments expressed at the luncheon are similar to those from the bridal shower, the remarks often have an informal feeling. If present, the proud mom might echo some of the thoughts behind her wedding shower toast.

BRIDE

This is the perfect time for the bride to share some private time with her girlfriends before tying the knot. She may even choose to give them their wedding party gifts during this event.

- Thank hardworking bridesmaids and maid/matron of honor for their help during the wedding preparations
- Express how much their friendship means to her
- Special thanks to mother, if present

This individual responds to the bride's toast on the bridesmaids' behalf. Additionally, each bridesmaid or friend present might like to add a personalized message.

- Thanks to bride for toast
- Thanks to bride or bride's mother for arranging lunch or activity
- May give bride humorous last-minute pre-wedding pep talk
- Toast to their friendship and a happily wedded life

The Bachelor/Bachelorette Party

The fact that these can be rowdy, raucous occasions comes as no surprise to anyone. The toasts associated with these two activities naturally follow suit. B-Parties that involve drinking, of course, increase the number of opportunities to toast the bride and groom, and non-wedding-party friends and relatives who also attend can join in the toast-a-thon (where they traditionally would not at the wedding reception). Unlike at other events, the bride and groom's past and future romantic lives seem to be fair fodder for toasting here.

The de facto host and hostess of these events should lead the toasting.

- Welcome to all in attendance
- A few words about their friendship and shared history with the groom and bride
- A humorous recap of the bride or groom's past romantic lives
- A tongue-in-cheek tribute to the passing of the bride or groom's singlehood

BRIDE/GROOM

Though this event is one spent surrounded by your closest friends, when it's time to toast, the bride or groom should remember to salute her or his future spouse.

- Thanks to organizer of party
- Thanks to bridal party for all their hard work
- A toast in absentia to his fiancée or her fiancé
- A few final words about the passing of singlehood

The Rehearsal Dinner

At one time restricted to close family members and the bridal party, the rehearsal celebration now commonly is opened to any guests who have traveled in from out of town. Oftentimes the rehearsal dinner can become a bit of a mini-reception in its own right, albeit a more casual one, complete with a toasting marathon.

HOSTS/PARENTS

As a counterpoint to the engagement party, the rehearsal dinner is traditionally hosted by the groom's parents, but in the event they cannot host, the bride's parents or the couple themselves may take on the role.

- Welcome and thanks to all in attendance
- Thanks to bridal party for an excellent rehearsal
- Reminiscences of the wedding planning process
- Humorous marriage advice
- Good luck and best wishes to the to-be-weds on their wedding day and always

BRIDE AND GROOM

Speaking together or separately, the bride and groom can take this opportunity to give their litany of thanks to all present and involved, and share their excitement for what lies before them.

- Thanks to hosts
- Thanks to all in attendance
- Thanks to bridal party
- Special thanks to both sets of parents
- A few words to each other
- Excitement and disbelief that the day is actually upon them
- Happiness at the joining of their two families

WEDDING PARTY MEMBERS

With the best man and maid of honor taking the lead, the whole wedding party might wish to propose a toast, either individually or as a group effort.

- Thanks to hosts
- Excitement at being part of the wedding
- "Behind the scenes" stories about the wedding planning or the rehearsal
- Last-minute advice for the ceremony
- Wishes for the couple

GRANDPARENTS

In the hustle and bustle of activity in the days leading up to the wedding day, these special people can sometimes be overlooked. The rehearsal dinner, in its smaller format, is an ideal place for Grandma or Grandpa to wax eloquent on subjects from their wealth of life experience.

- Reminiscences of bride and groom as children
- Their hopes for them then and now
- Their happiness at being able to witness the big day
- Lessons in love or marriage advice
- Good luck and best wishes to the to-be-weds on their wedding day and always

GUESTS

Sometimes, it seems like just about everyone has something to say! Chances are, several guests might also want to share their blessings. Encourage them to do so at the rehearsal dinner, rather than the reception when the course of events will inevitably be on a much tighter schedule.

- Brief introduction of who they are in relation to bride or groom
- Short and sweet toast with good wishes for the couple

Though they may have taken place many months before the actual wedding and reception, these toasts are no less important and will likely be memorable for entirely different reasons—the newness and nervousness the couple felt at their engagement party, the bonds of friendship at showers and bachelor/bachelorette parties, the excitement and adrenaline of the rehearsal dinner. Toast makers for these occasions might also wish to present the couple with a copy of their words for posterity.

What is love if not the language of the heart?

—ANONYMOUS

CHAPTER FOUR

WRITING A TOAST

ACTUALLY SITTING DOWN to write a toast that is meaningful and memorable might initially seem like a daunting task. It's not often that we are called to publicly proclaim heartfelt thoughts to our friends or even our family members. With words this important, it is necessary to be prepared. The best toasts are the ones where all the advance preparation makes the end result seem breezy and unrehearsed. Even if you are very talented at speaking off the cuff, nerves might kick in during your actual delivery, leaving you with your mouth open and guests wondering when to take a sip of champagne. Instead, thoroughly think through your toast beforehand, and allow plenty of time to perfect and practice your tribute. Plan to finish your toast a few weeks before the wedding—this will help alleviate some of the stress associated with preparing such a speech. If you feel like you need extra material, you can add in bits that relate to the days leading up to the wedding or even special moments from the ceremony at the last minute.

<hr />

Getting Started

Start by assembling whatever it is you need to collect your thoughts and organize your ideas—a notebook and pen, note cards, a laptop—and find a quiet corner where you can concentrate. Think about the tone you would like your toast to have—serious, sentimental, funny. You might wish to craft a combination toast, and take your audience on an emotional journey of humorous highs and tear-jerking reminiscences. Whichever track you choose, the goal is for your toast to be as personal as possible—it should sound like it was written especially for the person/s intended, and not a general statement that could apply to anyone. Keep this in mind as you begin to research and write your toast, and be sure to store all of your musings and any information you find in one place.

Doing Your Research

In this initial phase, you can make an outline or a list of key words and phrases to begin to bring your toast to life. Create category headings of the topics you want to cover (such as thanks, wedding planning stories, anecdotes, advice, and the like), then fill in the blanks as you go.

Collect your feelings about your toastee
The following questions might help get your creative juices flowing:

- When did you first meet? How long have you known each other?
- What stands out in your mind about your shared history together?
- What are some of your favorite memories together?
- Why is this person special to you?
- What do you admire about this person?
- Why is this person important in relation to the wedding?
- What are your wishes and hopes for this person?
- If you are toasting the bride and groom, how did you know it was love?
- What is great about their relationship?

Prepare your anecdotes
If you'd like to pepper your toast with amusing personal

stories, assemble your top ten funniest and most relevant tales, then narrow those down to your top three possibilities and see which fit best into the context of your toast.

Gather quotes and poems

If you are having trouble expressing how you feel in your own words, try consulting the collection of quotes and poems arranged by topic in Chapter Seven. A quote is a great way to start a toast—you can break in your audience at the beginning of your toast using a quote with a theme of marriage or love or set the tone with a humorous quote. A good quote can also help you "sum it all up" and end your toast with a bang. Beyond use in writing your toast, these quotes can inspire some general ideas and themes that you may wish to cover as well as help you get in the right frame of mind during toast-writing time.

All borrowed words should somehow relate to the toastee and the occasion—you can adapt them if necessary. Choose a quote you personally respond to, or one that makes you think of your toastee or is particularly appropriate to the person or situation. You might even choose a quote from a hero of the toastee. Look for some meaningful element, and let the quote inspire your thoughts.

When using a quote or poem, always be sure to credit the author ("Katharine Hepburn once said...") and do not try to pass off the words as your own—some may be more well known and beloved than you may realize. Furthermore, if you choose to excerpt a favorite story or poem, check the context to make certain the overall message of the work is a positive one.

Conduct some interviews

If you are delivering one of the main toasts, you can broaden the perspective beyond your own impressions of the toastee with a little help from others who know the person well. Talk to parents, siblings, other close family members, or friends and even coworkers or bosses to mine for funny stories or varied aspects of the toastee's life. If you are toasting the bride and groom, you may wish to do a little extra sleuthing. While you don't want to reveal the content to them, you could probe a bit to see if their wedding has a theme you could possibly incorporate into your toast. You can also inquire how many guests they are expecting so you can prepare yourself for the size of your audience.

Make the most of miscellany

If you're still in need of a little something to spice up or supplement your toast, consider incidental information. Look up what happened in the news or relevant moments in history based on the wedding date, the date the couple got engaged, or the date of the toastee's birth and draw parallels to the occasion. Other sources of interesting tidbits might include the toastee's horoscope, Chinese animal sign, or the meaning of his or her name. Word games might also be useful—try saying something about the toastee based on words starting with each letter of his or her name.

Putting Pen to Paper

Count on writing at least one, and probably two or three, drafts. Aside from remembering the overarching goal of an introduction, content, and conclusion (see page 2), try not to get too wrapped up in structure and grammar and perfecting each sentence from the get go. Write without worry and say everything you want to say in the first couple of versions—you will edit and revise later.

Start with the meat of your toast, the content. Having done your research and spent time reflecting on the toastee, you have gathered all of the bits and pieces— what is important about the person to you, memories, interviews, and the like. Now you just need to play with arranging these elements in the most logical order and

DO keep things relatively short. At the very most, your toast should run no more than five minutes. Any longer than that, and the audience might start to lose interest.

DON'T apologize at the beginning of your toast for your ineptitude in public speaking. This just starts your toast out on the wrong foot. If it would help you relax, it's OK to admit to the crowd you're feeling a bit nervous.

DO aim for a balance between sentiment and humor—be touching but not sappy.

DON'T use an overly dramatic speaking style or cliches. These types of language can make a toast seem stilted.

DO stay on target. Be mindful that the toast be about the toastee, not you, and always return the focus back to the person you are honoring. Watch for pronouns like "I" and "me" and "my" during the edit process.

DON'T make your toast an inside joke only a handful of people will understand.

stringing them together. It might be helpful to list or make a brief outline of everything you wish to cover.

Once you have a draft of your content, start scribing a worthy introduction. After you get through the particulars of who you are and your thanks for being a part of the proceedings, it's helpful to select a "hook" to set the tone and get everyone's attention before you proceed with the rest of your tribute. One of the best quotes, jokes, or stories you have collected could be your lead-in hook to the content of your toast. For example: "Good evening, everyone. For those of you who don't know me, I'm Will Cunningham, and I'm thrilled to serve as Oliver's best man. The writer Ring Lardner once wrote, 'They gave each other a smile with a future in it.' I want you all to know that I happened to be present at Princeton's freshman dance when Oliver first met Frances. And if the grins that passed between them that night are any indication, those words could have been written just for them."

As you write, be aware that many of the guests may not know both the bride and groom or both sets of parents. Your job as toast maker is to educate them. Be personal but not exclusionary in your language. "If I can share the following with you..." is a good way to introduce an anecdote and make everyone feel included. If you have been asked to deliver a toast and only know the bride or the groom very well yourself, it's fine to say so. For example, saying, "While I've only known Frances a short time, I have seen what an impact she has made on my friend Oliver's life" is honest but still honors both parties.

Edit your work in subsequent drafts. To refine your toast technically, look for logical transitions from one thought to the next, and aim for concise sentences so you can take natural pauses and breaths throughout. Be aware of refining you toast stylistically, too. Have a sense of your personal style and avoid trying to sound like something you're not—whether that is humorous, sentimental, or erudite—or your efforts will not come across as genuine. If you don't feel like something sounds like you or if you feel strange saying something out loud, delete or rework that passage. In addition, consider the style of the toastee—a toast should complement, not contrast or compete with, who a person is. For example, if the honoree is a quiet sort, a rollicking no-holds-barred toast will seem inappropriate. Make sure your language sounds right for the occasion as well as the person.

Polish and Edit

If you've said all you can say, it's time to tune your toast to perfect pitch. Decide what your final time limit for

A toast is made in the spirit of good cheer, and shouldn't offend or embarrass anyone. Off-color humor and controversial topics have no place in a wedding toast. Make sure what you choose to say is appropriate to the members of your audience—remember, there may be grandparents or children present. With these points in mind, the following sensitive subjects and themes are best avoided during a toast (and, most would agree, in polite company in general):

- embarrassing references to the wedding night or honeymoon
- ethnic jokes
- excessive discussion of past conquests
- ex spouses or previous serious partners
- outdated views on the roles of the sexes (e.g., a woman's place is in the kitchen, the man wears the pants in the relationship)
- politics
- profanity
- references to having children, in case the bride or groom is unable or the couple is not planning to
- religion
- ridiculing the wedding itself
- touchy subjects like money or power

the toast is going to be—most weddings experts rec-
ommend somewhere between three and five minutes in
length. Do a dry run of your toast out loud and time
yourself to see how far off you really are from your target time. Pay attention to any place you may have stum-
bled over your words and decide if any rewriting would
help. Next, start cutting. Edit out words that are super-
fluous or repetitive. Check that sentences are short and
clear. Delete any redundant thoughts or parts that
might, in retrospect, be too embarrassing to include.
Check your time again, and pare down further if necessary. What remains should be your very best material. If
you need to, leave your toast for a while and go back to
it later with a fresh perspective.

When you feel comfortable with what you have thus
far, seek assistance from an impartial co-editor to help
you polish your final toast. Choose someone honest
with an impeccable ear, and deliver your toast in all its
glory to him or her. Ask for constructive criticism on
your tone, topics, and overall delivery. If you don't have
anyone who can help you out, tape yourself giving the
toast, then be your own judge.

After editing and critique, you can set up your speaking
notes. For the most natural delivery, you want some
notes to refer to but not something you will read word
for word. Even if you feel comfortable enough to mem-

orize your toast completely, having something in your hand to fall back on is advisable. Use whatever format is easiest for you: an outline with key words and phrases, prose with important words and topics highlighted, or main topics dissected into sections on note cards.

Rehearse

Practice, as they say, makes perfect. With speaking notes in hand, rehearse your toast out loud so you become comfortable with the language and familiar with the content. In front of a mirror is good, but in front of a live audience (perhaps your impartial judge from before) is better. Alternatively, you might even want to film yourself to review your performance.

While you practice, get a sense of where the natural breaks are in your toast; actually writing "PAUSE" in your speaking notes can help make sure you don't miss your opportunity to take a breath or wait for audience response. And, as in any public speaking situation, watch out for clumsy filler like "you know" and "um" in your speech patterns. Listen to the tempo and pitch of your voice and be aware of sounding too high or in a monotone. If this sounds like a lot to remember, it becomes easier the more you practice.

Feeling some pre-toast anxiety? It's perfectly normal. A classic way to de-stress is to visualize yourself giving your toast clearly and confidently; it's the power of positive thinking—if you envision yourself giving a good toast, you will give a good toast. If you are especially nervous about your delivery, try to make an advance visit to the location where you will be toasting to get an idea of the size and acoustics of the room. As a final preparation, make an extra copy or two of your toast, and give it to other people attending the festivities in case you misplace your own copy.

To love someone deeply gives you strength.
Being loved by someone deeply gives you courage.
— LAO TZU

CHAPTER FIVE

DELIVERING A TOAST

ONCE YOUR TOASTING day of reckoning arrives, try to relax and not let it dominate your thoughts so you can enjoy yourself. If you have butterflies in your stomach, remember that everyone present is cheering you on and excited to hear what you have to say. After all, weddings and their related festivities are joyful occasions, and even if by chance you do slip up somehow, you will be all the more endeared to your audience. Also make sure to take a look at Chapter Six on the etiquette of toasting to make sure you're set for the big day.

Before Your Toast

Your preparation is just as important as your actual proposing of the toast. Before you stand and deliver, consider the following:

Remember to eat something
You'll need your energy, and you won't be distracted by a grumbling stomach mid-toast.

Give yourself a once over
Sneak a peak in a compact mirror or make a quick trip to the restroom to double check your appearance. Toasts are prime photo-taking opportunities, and you'll want to look your best for posterity and make sure those in the front row won't be focusing on that bit of spinach in your teeth instead of your heartfelt tribute.

Find a friendly face or two
If you're nervous, making eye contact and focusing on people you know in the room will make you feel more comfortable. Before you take the stage, look around and identify where a few of these safety nets are sitting.

Make yourself heard
Perform a brief test on the microphone to avoid static and buzzing, and to check the volume level. You might

wish to arrange for someone such as a wedding planner to stand in the back of the room and indicate whether or not you are audible. Ideally, the microphone will be in a stand so you don't have to juggle it along with your notes and your drink. If there is no microphone, make sure you project your voice out into the audience.

⮞ TOASTS AROUND THE WORLD

Give your toast a cultural connection based on the couple's heritage, the location of the wedding, or the destination of the honeymoon.

Brazil *Saúde*

England *Cheers*

France *A votre santé*

Germany *Prosit*

Greece *Eis Ighian*

India *Jaikind*

Ireland *Sláinte*

Israel *L'Chaim*

Italy *Salute*

Japan *Kanpai*

Mexico *Salud*

Russia *Na zdorovia*

Spain *Salud*

Sweden *Skål*

Have beverage, will toast
Since you are leading the toast, be sure you have a drink in your hand or at least in your vicinity for when you are finished speaking. That being said, don't have too much to drink prior to proposing a toast. Have a glass beforehand to calm your nerves if necessary, but not so many that you are slurring your words. And remember, you don't have to toast with an alcoholic beverage at all; you can use sparkling water, fruit juice, or a soft drink (just don't toast with a cup of tea or coffee).

During Your Toast

Once you take center stage all eyes are on you. Whether you are speaking before a handful of friends at a bachelor or bachelorette party or two hundred people at the reception, a few simple rules apply:

Take a stand
Standing commands the attention of your audience and helps you project your voice. To put the focus on you, stand confidently at your full height. If possible, speak in front of a flat surface like a podium where you can rest your notes or drink if need be.

The classic beverage for toasting is champagne, but you might be inspired to raise a glass of something different based on the locale where the wedding takes place, the cultural background of the bride and groom or even a favored drink of their preference.

BEER: Belgium, England, Germany, Ireland, Mexico

CAMPARI: Italy

GIN: England, The Netherlands

OUZO: Greece

PASTIS: France

PIMM'S: England

RUM: Caribbean, Cuba, Jamaica

SAKE: Japan

TEQUILA: Mexico

VODKA: Finland, Poland, Russia, Sweden

WHISKEY: Ireland, Kentucky, Scotland

WINE: Argentina, Australia, Austria, California, Chile, France, Germany, Greece, Italy, New Zealand, Portugal, South Africa, Spain

Start with a smile

It's a celebration, not a funeral. Smiling immediately sets the tone for your toast and will help you relax.

Look them in the eye

Establish eye contact with the person or persons you are toasting; your gaze can then rove and settle on assorted members of the audience while you are relaying a story or giving advice, but be sure to return to and maintain eye contact with the individual/s you are honoring during the actual toast.

Speak up

Give your toast confidently, loudly and clearly. Slow down and take your time so people can understand you and let it all sink in.

Now breathe

You are not under water, so be sure to keep breathing. Breathe and make logical breaks in your speech, both for emphasis and to help you keep your composure. It's OK to take an extra couple of seconds during pauses so you can catch your breath.

Mind your language

You of course know that curse words and innuendo are off limits, but don't forget to mind your body language, too. Try to control fidgeting or fussing too much, and avoid shuffling your feet, playing with your hair or tie, and jingling things in your pocket. All are distractions for you and your audience.

Be in touch with your emotions

During your toast, you may find yourself getting a little choked up over the sentiments you've expressed. If this happens, stop for a moment and take a couple of breaths or sips of water to pull yourself together before carrying on. No one will think ill of your toasting abilities, and in fact a few others may be reaching for a tissue. Similarly, if you make a mistake or lose your place, simply stop, correct yourself, and continue.

Let the good times roll

If something funny you've crafted generates a big laugh from the audience, just smile, enjoy the moment your words have brought, and wait for the noise to die down before you continue.

Go out with a bang

Don't lose steam before your big finish. While your anecdotes were great for garnering a few chuckles from guests, they weren't the main message of your toast. Be sure that when you are actually ready to raise your glass you can muster the momentum to end your toast on an energetic upswing. You'll be all the more memorable for it.

~~~~~~

After Your Toast

Now that you've said your piece, you can relax and enjoy yourself knowing that you have contributed to the memories and fun of a joyous occasion. Now quietly say, "cheers!" to yourself, and take another sip in honor of a job well done!

Never above you.
Never below you. Always beside you.
— WALTER WINCHELL

CHAPTER SIX

TOAST ETIQUETTE

LIKE MANY ASPECTS of a wedding, toasting comes
complete with its own set of rules and regulations, and,
more specifically, an etiquette. This especially holds
true for reception toasts where the level of formality of
a wedding and the number of guests help determine
when a toast should be made.

For the most formal weddings, toasting at the reception occurs after guests have concluded the entire meal.
If the wedding cake will be served as dessert, the toasting can begin after the cutting of the cake. Less formally, toasting may begin once everyone has been
seated and served drinks. To break things up a bit,
toasts can be proposed in between the courses of the
meal if there are several to be made. This idea of multi-

ple toasts at different points during the reception has become very popular. No matter what approach is taken, everyone who is giving a toast should be aware of their place in the lineup and be ready to go when it's their turn.

The traditional order for toasts at a formal reception would be as follows: the bride's father, the groom, and the best man. A more contemporary variation would also include the bride's mother, the bride, and the maid of honor. Alternatively, for some less formal receptions the toasts commence with the best man, followed by the groom and his bride (together or separately), the maid of honor, and the fathers or parents of the newlyweds. In all scenarios, an emcee or toastmaster (see below) would introduce each person making a toast and assist in keeping things moving in the desired order.

There are four core participants in almost every wedding toast: a toastmaster, the toaster who actually delivers the toast, the toastee (the recipient of the toast), and the audience of all those present.

~~~~~~

The Toastmaster

Although the term is somewhat antiquated, the toastmaster has an important job. He or she essentially runs

the show and keeps things moving smoothly by intro-
ducing all those planning to speak.

WHO

It is a tradition in the United Kingdom to hire a profes-
sional toastmaster to manage the toast flow and other
social necessities of a wedding such as announcing the
receiving line. However, in the United States it is perfectly acceptable to ask your bandleader or DJ to serve
in this capacity. The best man or maid-of-honor also
commonly take on this role, and some wedding plan-
ners will include toastmaster as one of their responsi-
bilities. Prior to the reception, the toastmaster should
be provided with a list of the names of the specific individuals who will be toasting (along with the pronuncia-
tions of their names), the order in which the toasts will
be given, and a schedule outlining points during the reception when the toasts will be made.

HOW

To get the ball rolling, the toastmaster must first get
the group's attention. In some circles, tapping on a
glass with a spoon is the call to pay attention as the
toasting begins. (Note: This is not always a safe practice, as rigorous striking just might break the glass, and

this method is frowned upon in general by certain pro-
tocol mavens.) If the reception is small and being held
in a fairly intimate setting, the toastmaster may be able
to simply stand with a raised glass until everyone's attention is captured. Alternatively, the toastmaster
could ask the band or DJ to play some kind of introduc-
tory music or simply stand at the microphone and announce, "May I have your attention, please?"

ᢕᢖᢗ TOASTING TIPS FOR SECOND MARRIAGES

Many second marriages have celebrations that rival the
first, complete with tiered cake, white wedding gown, two-
hundred plus reception guest list, and, of course, toasts.
Making a toast under these circumstances may require
some degree of tact and consideration, and if you have
been called upon to deliver a toast be sensitive in your
choice of words. For example, it is acceptable to mention
the couple's respective kids in the toast, but it's in poor
taste to mention the bride or groom's previous marriage.
While you cannot ignore their history, you can look forward to their new life together and comment upon the
couple's future with broad statements about how they
found each other, how their marriage is worth the wait,
that they are entertaining a new chapter of their lives, or
how their love is a triumph of hope over experience.

The Toast Maker

All eyes and ears are on the toast maker as he or she is announced by the toastmaster before rising to deliver the toast.

WHO

As already noted, while no one is required to give a toast, the primary toasters at a wedding reception generally may include: The bride and groom, the bride's father, the best man, and the maid of honor. All toasters should be asked by or receive permission from the bride and groom to toast.

HOW

Anyone giving a toast should stand. In smaller settings, a toaster may simply stand at his or her place at the table to deliver the toast. In larger environments, the toaster should take the floor at a microphone in order to be heard by all. When toasting, be sure you remember to have a beverage in your hand, or at least nearby. After you have said your piece, ask everyone to stand and join you as you raise your glass in honor of the toastee and take a sip. If you have toasted the newlywed couple, it's a thoughtful gesture to present them with a

If we haven't witnessed one before ourselves, we've heard about one from a friend or a friend of a friend—the truly awful toast. Perhaps the offender is a windbag relative who has had a few too many drinks or old "friend" whose jealousy didn't rear its ugly head till it was time to make a toast. Here's how to handle a less-than-stellar toast.

❧ *THE BURNT TOAST*

While rare, a seemingly innocent toast might take a turn for the worse and end up sounding more like a roast or an all-out character assassination, a litany of ex-loves of the bride or groom, or other assorted nastiness.

How to avoid it
While you won't always know what evil lurks in the heart of a renegade toaster, you can head off potential turncoats at the pass. Discuss with the toastmaster beforehand who is and who isn't expected and invited to toast, and if you suspect a potential toaster might have something up his or her proverbial sleeve make sure they are on the "No Toast" list. The toastmaster should have the official list and announce each toaster—and head off any undesirables before they ever make it to the mike.

If you are the recipient of this kind of toast, don't let it upset you, even if the errant toaster has made incendiary or insensitive remarks. The only one who looks like a fool is the toaster. If things start to turn sour, your toastmaster or emcee should intercede, reclaim the microphone, and cut the toast short.

∾ THE NEVER-ENDING TOAST

Are guests yawning or checking their watches? When a toast sounds more like a filibuster or long-play monologue, the toaster has gone too far.

How to avoid it

When you invite someone with a proclivity towards the verbose to toast, ask them to say, "a few words, no more than a minute or two" to try to control their urge to go into overtime.

If it happens

Make sure your toastmaster knows he or she has the power—and your blessing—to step in and reclaim the microphone when the toaster takes a breath with a gentle "OK, thank you for your kind words, Uncle Fred, but let's give someone else a chance to wish the happy couple well."

copy of the toast you delivered to keep with their wedding mementos.

The Toastee

The lucky recipients of a toast, the toastees have their own set of protocols to follow.

WHO

A wedding toastee can be the bride and groom (as a couple or individually), the bride's parents, the groom's parents, the bridesmaids and anyone in the wedding party, and even the guests.

HOW

If you are being toasted to, remain seated and do not raise your glass or drink from it during the toast. Once everyone else has taken a sip, you may join them by drinking from your glass. Some brides and grooms choose to interlock their arms when taking a sip to signify the joining of their two lives; this requires some degree of coordination from both parties, who may want to practice their moves prior to the wedding to prevent champagne stains on the wedding attire.

Once the toaster has finished, the toastee generally follows with a toast of his or her own and is responsible for making some kind of response acknowledging the kind words of the toaster. For example a groom could say, "Thanks to my big brother Tim for making me shed a few tears—though this time it's from the beautiful toast, not stealing all of my toys." With an eye to etiquette, some proper responses include that of the groom to the father of the bride and/or the best man, the best man on behalf of the bridesmaids to the groom, and the bride to the groom.

Present Company

Anyone who is part of the audience for a toast should listen for the duration and follow along with any requests from the toaster (e.g., "Please stand and join me..."). No one at the celebration should ever refuse to toast; if someone does not drink alcohol, it is perfectly acceptable to forgo the champagne or wine offered and substitute a non-alcoholic beverage.

Love is composed of a single soul
inhabiting two bodies.

— ARISTOTLE

CHAPTER SEVEN

WORDS TO INSPIRE

THE FOLLOWING is a selection of quotes, pithy as well as poignant, on topics which might come in handy when writing a toast. Their purpose here is to inspire — use them as they are or adapt them at your will, just be sure to acknowledge the person who originally said or wrote the words and give credit where credit is due. Though the quotes are arranged by general categories for ease, you may choose freely among them regardless of your role in the toasting proceedings. Beyond their value for toasts, they can be used to personalize printed materials such as programs and thank you notes.

Love

The heart can do anything.

— MOLIÈRE

Love cannot be forced.
Love cannot be coaxed and teased.
It comes out of Heaven,
Unasked and unsought.

— PEARL S. BUCK

Love is what you've been through with somebody.

— JAMES THURBER

Love is an act of endless forgiveness, a tender look
which becomes a habit.

— PETER USTINOV

Love does not consist in gazing at each other but in
looking together in the same direction.

— ANTOINE DE SAINT-EXUPÉRY

Love means giving one's self to another person fully, not
just physically. When two people really love each other,
this helps them to stay alive and grow. One must really
be loved to grow. Love's such a precious and fragile

thing that when it comes we have to hold on tightly. And when it comes, we're very lucky because for some it never comes at all. If you have love, you're wealthy in a way that can never be measured. Cherish it.

— NANCY REAGAN

The love we give away is the only love we keep.

— ELBERT HUBBARD

The love we have in our youth is superficial compared to the love that an old man has for his old wife.

— WILL DURANT

The true beloveds of this world are in their lover's eyes lilacs opening, ship lights, school bells, a landscape, re-membered conversations, friends, a child's Sunday, lost voices, one's favorite suit, autumn and all seasons, memory, yes, it being the earth and water of existence, memory.

— TRUMAN CAPOTE

This being in love is great—you get a lot of compli-ments and begin to think you are a great guy.

— F. SCOTT FITZGERALD

From *How to Save Your Own Life*
ERICA JONG

Do you want me to tell you something really subversive? Love is everything it's cracked up to be. That's why people are so cynical about it....It really IS worth fighting for, being brave, for risking everything for...And the trouble is, if you don't risk anything, you risk even MORE.

They gave each other a smile with a future in it.

—RING LARDNER

We cannot really love anybody with whom we never laugh.

—AGNES REPPLIER

The greatest happiness of life is the conviction that we are loved—loved for ourselves, or rather, in spite of ourselves.

—VICTOR HUGO

Every wedding where true lovers wed, helps on the march of universal love.

—HERMAN MELVILLE

Love gives naught but itself and takes naught but from itself. Love possesses not nor would it be possessed; For love is sufficient unto love.

— KAHLIL GIBRAN

Perhaps the feelings that we experience when we are in love represent a normal state. Being in love shows a person who he should be.

— ANTON CHEKHOV

Age does not protect you from love. But love, to some extent, protects you from age.

— JEANNE MOREAU

It's not good trying to fool yourself about love. You can't fall into it like a soft job, without dirtying up your hands. It takes muscle and guts. And if you can't bear the thought of messing up your nice, clean soul, you'd better give up the whole idea of life, and become a saint. Because you'll never make it as a human being. It's either this world or the next.

— JOHN OSBORNE

When you love someone all your saved-up wishes start coming out.

— ELIZABETH BOWEN

Your success and happiness lie in you.

— HELEN KELLER

Where there is love, there is life.

— GANDHI

Where there is great love there are always miracles.

— WILLA CATHER

Love is a fire that feeds our life.

— PABLO NERUDA

There is nothing more lovely in life than the union of two people whose love for one another has grown through the years from the small acorn of passion into a great-rooted tree.

— VITA SACKVILLE-WEST

Love is not a matter of counting the years, it is making the years count. Love is the master key that opens the gates of happiness.

— OLIVER WENDELL HOLMES

If I know what love is, it is because of you.

— HERMANN HESSE

Love is of all passions the strongest, for it attacks simultaneously the head, the heart, and the senses.

—VOLTAIRE

To be loved, be lovable.

—OVID

We are all born for love. It is the principle of existence and its only end.

—BENJAMIN DISRAELI

Love conquers all.

—VIRGIL

To love a person means to agree to grow old with him.

—ALBERT CAMUS

I love you for what you are, but I love you yet more for what you are going to be.

—CARL SANDBURG

Your words dispel all of the care in the world and make me happy...They are as necessary to me now as sunlight and air...your words are my food, your breath my wine—you are everything to me.

—SARAH BERNHARDT

Love is a portion of the soul itself, and it is of the same nature as the celestial breathing of the atmosphere of paradise.

—VICTOR HUGO

When one has only fully entered the realm of love, the world—no matter how imperfect—becomes rich and beautiful and consists solely of opportunity.

— SØREN KIERKEGAARD

There is only one happiness in life, to love and be loved.

— GEORGE SAND

We are shaped and fashioned by what we love.

—JOHANN WOLFGANG VON GOETHE

Love is not a union merely between two creatures, it is a union between two spirits.

—FREDERICK W. ROBERTSON

There is only one terminal dignity—love. And the story of a love is not important—what is important is that one is capable of love. It is perhaps the only glimpse we are permitted of eternity.

— HELEN HAYES

Love recognizes no barriers. It jumps hurdles, leaps fences, and penetrates walls to arrive at its destination full of hope.

—MAYA ANGELOU

Love has nothing to do with what you are expecting to get. Only what you are expecting to give, which is everything.

—KATHARINE HEPBURN

It was not into my ear you whispered but into my heart.

—JUDY GARLAND

I love you because you are you.

—MICHEL EYQUEM DE MONTAIGNE

Love is much nicer to be in than an automobile accident, a tight girdle, a higher tax bracket, or a holding pattern over Philadelphia.

—JUDITH VIORST

Love is a fire. But whether it is going to warm your hearth or burn down your house, you can never tell.

—JOAN CRAWFORD

Here's to the happy man: All the world loves a lover.

—RALPH WALDO EMERSON

Oh, hasten not this living act,
Rapture where self and not-self meet:
My life has been the awaiting you,
Your footfall was my own heart's beat.

— PAUL VALÉRY

To love is to suffer. To avoid suffering one must not love. But then one suffers from not loving. Therefore, to love is to suffer; not to love is to suffer; to suffer is to suffer. To be happy is to love. To be happy, then, is to suffer, but suffering makes one unhappy. Therefore, to be happy one must love or love to suffer or suffer from too much happiness.

— WOODY ALLEN

~~~~~~

Brides and Grooms

From *To a Bride*
FRANCIS QUARLES

Let all thy joys be as the month of May
And all thy days be as a marriage day:
Let sorrow, sickness, and a troubled mind
Be stranger to thee.

To the man who has conquered the bride's heart—and her mother's!

—ANONYMOUS

A toast to the groom—and discretion to his bachelor friends!

—ANONYMOUS

~~~~~~

Husbands and Wives

When a man makes a woman his wife, it's the highest compliment he can pay her, and it's usually the last.

<div align="right">—HELEN ROWLAND</div>

American women expect to find in their husbands a perfection that English women only hope to find in their butlers.

<div align="right">—SOMERSET MAUGHAM</div>

Bachelor: A peacock; betrothed: a lion; married: a donkey

<div align="right">—SPANISH PROVERB</div>

There are two kinds of marriages—where the husband quotes the wife, or where the wife quotes the husband.

<div align="right">—CLIFFORD ODETS</div>

Wives and watermelons are picked by chance.

—GREEK PROVERB

I've had the boyhood thing of being Elvis. Now I want to be with my best friend, and my best friend is my wife. Who could ask for anything more?

—JOHN LENNON

Meek wifehood is no part of my profession; I am your friend, but never your possession.

—VERA BRITTAIN

I chose my wife as she did her wedding gown, not for a fine glossy surface, but such qualities that would age well.

—OLIVER GOLDSMITH

My most brilliant achievement was my ability to be able to persuade my wife to marry me.

—WINSTON CHURCHILL

A happy marriage has in it all the pleasures of friendships, all the enjoyment of sense and reason—and indeed all the sweets of life.

—JOSEPH ADDISON

One never realizes how different a husband and wife
can be until they begin to pack for a trip.

—ERMA BOMBECK

Take each other for better or worse but not for granted.

—ARLENE DAHL

To My Dear and Loving Husband
ANNE BRADSTREET

If ever two were one, then surely we.
If ever man were loved by wife, then thee;
If ever wife was happy in a man,
Compare with me, ye women, if you can.
I prize thy love more than whole mines of gold
Or all the riches that the East doth hold.
My love is such that rivers cannot quench,
Nor ought but love from thee, give recompense.
Thy love is such I can no way repay,
The heavens reward thee manifold, I pray.
Then while we live, in love let's so persevere
That when we live no more, we may live ever.

Couples

If we are a metaphor of the universe, the human couple is the metaphor par excellence, the point of intersection of all forces and the seed of all forms. The couple is time recaptured, and the return to the time before time.

—OCTAVIO PAZ

The meeting of two personalities is like the contract of two chemical substances: if there is any reaction, both are transformed.

—CARL JUNG

Apache Wedding Prayer

Now you will feel no rain,
For each of you will be shelter to the other.
Now you will feel no cold,
For each of you will be warmth to the other.
Now there is no more loneliness,
For each of you will be companion to the other.
Now you are two bodies,
But there is only one life before you.
Go now to your dwelling place
To enter into the days of your togetherness
And may your days be good and long upon the earth.

Cool breeze
Warm fire
Full moon
Easy chair
Empty plates
Soft words
Sweet songs
Tall tales
Short sips
Long life

—JOHN EGERTON

Everything comes to us from others. To be is to belong to someone.

—JEAN-PAUL SARTRE

From the *Odyssey*
HOMER

There is nothing nobler or more admirable than when two people who see eye to eye keep house as man and wife, confounding their enemies and delighting their friends.

Everybody has to be somebody to somebody to be anybody.

—MALCOLM FORBES

One of the oldest human needs is having someone to wonder where you are when you don't come home at night.

—MARGARET MEAD

The greatest of all the arts is the art of living together.

—WILLIAM LYON PHELPS

Destiny
SIR EDWIN ARNOLD

Somewhere there waiteth in this world of ours
For one lone soul another lonely soul,
Each choosing each through all the weary hours
And meeting strangely at one sudden goal.
Then blend they, like green leaves with golden flowers,
Into one beautiful and perfect whole;
And life's long night is ended, and the way
Lies open onward to eternal day.

What greater thing is there for two human souls than to feel that they are joined...to strengthen each other...to be at one with each other in silent unspeakable memories.

—GEORGE ELIOT

Friends and Friendship

What is commonly called friendship is only a little more honor among rogues.

—HENRY DAVID THOREAU

Let us be grateful to people who make us happy; they are the charming gardeners who make our souls blossom.

—MARCEL PROUST

Your friend is the man who knows all about you, and still likes you.

—ELBERT HUBBARD

There are good ships and bad ships, but the best ships are friendships.

—ANONYMOUS

Many people walk in and out of your life, but only true friends will leave footprints in your heart.

—ELEANOR ROOSEVELT

My best friend is the one who brings out the best in me.

—HENRY FORD

There is no possession more valuable than a good and faithful friend.

— SOCRATES

May the friends of our youth be the companions of our old age.

— ANONYMOUS

Here's to eternity—may we spend it in as good company as this night finds us.

— ANONYMOUS

Among those whom I like, I can find no common denominator, but among those I love, I can; all of them make me laugh.

— W. H. AUDEN

A real friend is one who walks in when the rest of the world walks out.

— WALTER WINCHELL

To my best friend's new best friend

— ANONYMOUS

Some friends come and go, but you are the truest friend I know.

— ELSA MAXWELL

Never shall I forget the days I spent with you. Continue to be my friend, as you will always find me yours.

—LUDWIG VAN BEETHOVEN

To the ladies, God bless them, may nothing distress them.

—ANONYMOUS

Happiness

Do not the most moving moments of our lives find us all without words?

—MARCEL MARCEAU

True happiness consists not in the multitude of friends, but in the worth and choice.

—BEN JONSON

Where your pleasure is, there is your treasure; where your treasure, there your heart; where your heart, there your happiness.

—SAINT AUGUSTINE

Marriage

Matrimony: The high sea for which no compass has yet been invented.

— HEINRICH HEINE

Marriage is like twirling a baton, turning handsprings, or eating with chopsticks. It looks so easy till you try it.

— HELEN ROWLAND

Marriage is the only known example of the happy meeting of the immovable object and the irresistible force.

— OGDEN NASH

To keep your marriage brimming
with love in the loving cup,
whenever you're wrong, admit it,
whenever you're right, shut up.

— OGDEN NASH

The great secret of successful marriage is to treat all disasters as incidents and none of the incidents as disasters.

— HAROLD NICOLSON

Chains do not hold a marriage together. It is threads, hundreds of tiny threads, which sew people together through the years. That is what makes a marriage last— more than passion or even sex!

— SIMONE SIGNORET

From *The Master Speed*
ROBERT FROST

Two such as you with such a master speed
cannot be parted nor be swept away
From one another once you are agreed
That life is only life forevermore
Together wing to wing and oar to oar

Marriage is not just spiritual communion and passionate embraces; marriage is also three meals a day and remember to carry out the trash.

— JOYCE BROTHERS

A successful marriage requires falling in love many times, always with the same person.

— MIGNON MCLAUGHLIN

There is no more lovely, friendly, and charming relationship, communion, or company than a good marriage.

—MARTIN LUTHER

Marriage Advice
JANE WELLS

Let your love be stronger than your hate and anger.
Learn the wisdom of compromise,
for it is better to bend a little than to break.
Believe the best rather than the worst.
People have a way of living up or down
to your opinion of them.
Remember that true friendship
is the basis for any lasting relationship.
The person you choose to marry
is deserving of the courtesies
and kindnesses you bestow on your friends.
Please hand this down to your children and
your children's children.

You don't marry one person; you marry three: the person you think they are, the person they are, and the person they are going to become as the result of being married to you.

—RICHARD NEEDHAM

Never go to bed angry. Stay up and fight.

— PHYLLIS DILLER

There is no secret to long marriage—it's hard work. It's serious business, and certainly not for cowards.

— OSSIE DAVIS

Keep your eyes wide open before marriage, half shut afterwards.

— BENJAMIN FRANKLIN

The world has grown suspicious of anything that looks like a happy married life.

— OSCAR WILDE

The key to a happy marriage is to remember those three little words, "You're right dear."

— ANONYMOUS

Never, never, never, never give up.

— WINSTON CHURCHILL

When we first got married, we made a pact. It was this: In our life together, it was decided that I would make all of the big decisions and my wife would make all of the little decisions. For fifty years, we have held true to that agreement. I believe that is the reason for the success in our marriage. However, the strange thing is that in fifty years, there hasn't been one big decision.

—ALBERT EINSTEIN, *on the occasion of his fiftieth wedding anniversary when asked about the success of his marriage*

Seek a happy marriage with the wholeness of heart, but do not expect to reach the promised land without going through some wilderness together.

—CHARLIE W. SHEDD

The real marriage of true minds is for any two people to possess a sense of humor or irony pitched in exactly the same key, so that their joint glances on any subject cross like interacting searchlights.

—EDITH WHARTON

A good marriage is that in which each appoints the other guardian of his solitude.

—RAINER MARIA RILKE

To marry is to halve your rights and double your duties.

—ARTHUR SCHOPENHAUER

The best way to remember your wedding anniversary is to forget it once.

—ANONYMOUS

The best part of married life is the fights. The rest is merely so-so.

— THORNTON WILDER

Marriage is the alliance of two people, one of whom never remembers birthdays, and the other who never forgets.

— OGDEN NASH

Our marriage works because we each carry clubs of equal weight and size.

— PAUL NEWMAN

The proper basis for marriage is mutual misunderstanding.

— OSCAR WILDE

The sum which two married people owe to one another defies calculation. It is an infinite debt, which can only be discharged through all eternity.

— JOHANN WOLFGANG VON GOETHE

The best marriages, like the best lives, were both happy and unhappy. There was even a kind of necessary tension, a certain tautness between the partners that gave the marriage strength, like the tautness of a full sail.

— ANNE MORROW LINDBERGH

Men and Women

The hardest task of a girl's life is to prove to a man that his intentions are serious.

— HELEN ROWLAND

A man in love is incomplete until he has married—then he is finished!

— ZSA ZSA GABOR

If you want to know about a man you can find out an awful lot by looking at who he married.

— KIRK DOUGLAS

I never liked the men I loved, and never loved the men I liked.

—FANNY BRICE in NORMAN KATKOV'S
The Fabulous Fanny

The moment my eyes fell on him, I was content.

— EDITH WHARTON

It's a funny thing that when a man hasn't got anything on earth to worry about, he goes off and gets married.

— ROBERT FROST

If you want to sacrifice the admiration of many men for the criticism of one, go ahead, get married.

— KATHARINE HEPBURN

A beauty is a woman you notice; A charmer is one who notices you.

— ADLAI STEVENSON

A wise woman puts a grain of sugar into everything she says to a man, and takes a grain of salt with everything he says to her.

— HELEN ROWLAND

Never try to impress a woman, because if you do, she'll expect you to keep up the standard for the rest of your life.

— W. C. FIELDS

Here's to the lasses we've loved, my lad
Here's to the lips we've pressed;
For of kisses and lasses,
Like liquor in glasses,
The last is always the best

— ANONYMOUS

Infatuation is when you think that he's as sexy as Robert Redford, as smart as Henry Kissinger, as noble as Ralph Nader, as funny as Woody Allen, and as ath-letic as Jimmy Connors. Love is when you realize that he's as sexy as Woody Allen, as smart as Jimmy Con-nors, as funny as Ralph Nader, as athletic as Henry Kissinger, and nothing like Robert Redford—but you'll take him anyway.

—JUDITH VIORST

Whatever our souls are made of, his and mine are the same.

—EMILY BRONTË

~~~~~~

Brothers and Sisters

There is only one good substitute for the endearments of a sister, and that is the endearments of some other fellow's sister.

—JOSH BILLINGS

There were two brothers who were smart and a third who got married.

—POLISH PROVERB

Big sisters are the crabgrass in the lawn of life.

—LINUS from CHARLES SCHULZ's *Peanuts*

Mothers and Fathers

Men are what their mothers made them.

— RALPH WALDO EMERSON

Blessed indeed is the man who hears many gentle voices call him father.

— LYDIA M. CHILD

All that I am or hope to be, I owe to my angel mother.

— ABRAHAM LINCOLN

A mother is the truest friend we have.

— WASHINGTON IRVING

Blessed are the mothers, for they have...pointed little eyes to the stars and little souls to eternal things.

— WILLIAM L. STIDGER

Oh the love of a mother, love which none can forget.

— VICTOR HUGO

My mother had a great deal of trouble with me, but I think she enjoyed it.

— MARK TWAIN

The most meaningful gift a father can give his children
is to love their mother.

—ANONYMOUS

Sons and Daughters

A Wedding Toast
RICHARD WILBUR

St. John tells how, at Cana's wedding feast,
The water-pots poured wine in such amount that by
    his sober count
There were a hundred gallons at the least.

It made no earthly sense, unless to show
How whatsoever love elects to bless
Brims to a sweet excess
That can without depletion overflow.

Which is to say that what love sees is true;
That the world's fullness is not made but found.
Life hungers to abound
And pour its plenty out for such as you.

Now, if your loves will lend an ear to mine,
I toast you both, good son and dear new daughter.
May you not lack for water,
And may that water smack of Cana's wine.

There are only two lasting bequests we can hope to give
our children. One of these is roots, the other wings.

—HODDING CARTER

I have found the best way to give advice to my children
is to find out what they want and then advise them to
do it.

—HARRY S. TRUMAN

You don't choose your family. They are God's gift to
you.

—DESMOND TUTU

~~~~~~

Wishes and Advice

May you live all the days of your life.

—JONATHAN SWIFT

We do not remember days, we remember moments.

—CESARE PAVESE

Yesterday is history, tomorrow is mystery...today is a gift.

— ELEANOR ROOSEVELT

Iroquois Tribal Wish

May you have a safe tent
And no sorrow as you travel.
May happiness attend you in all your paths.
May you keep a heart like the morning,
And may you come slow to the four corners
Where man says goodnight

Sing and dance together and be joyous, but let each
    one of you be alone,
Even as the strings of a lute are alone though they
    quiver with the same music.
Give your hearts, but not into each other's keeping
For only the hand of Life can contain your hearts.
And stand together yet not too near together:
For the pillars of the temple stand apart,
And the oak tree and the cypress grow not in each
    other's shadow.

— KAHLIL GIBRAN

A journey of a thousand miles begins with a single step.

— LAO TZU

May your joy never end like the circles of your wedding rings.

—ANONYMOUS

To love, laughter, and happily ever after.

—ANONYMOUS

May your love be modern enough to survive the times, and old-fashioned enough to last forever.

—ANONYMOUS

Let there be space in your togetherness.

— KAHLIL GIBRAN

Here's to the new husband
And here's to the new wife
May they remain lovers
For all of life.

—ANONYMOUS

May thy life be long and happy,
Thy cares and sorrows few;
And the many friends around thee
Prove faithful, fond and true.

—ANONYMOUS

Go confidently in the direction of your dreams!
Live the life you've imagined!

— HENRY DAVID THOREAU

Life is worth the living of it. Do it with your whole
heart.

— MAYA ANGELOU

May you always look into each other's eyes as you did
the night you first met.

— ANONYMOUS

Chinese Blessing

Ten thousand things bright
Ten thousand miles, no dust
Water and sky one color
Houses shining along your road.

As you make your way through life together, hold fast
to your dreams and each other's hands.

— ANONYMOUS

Live for the future
Learn from the past,
And enjoy the present.

— ANONYMOUS

May your hands be forever clasped in friendship and your hearts forever joined in love.

—ANONYMOUS

Here's to your future, your present and your past; may each new day be happier than the last.

—ANONYMOUS

I am beginning to learn that it is the sweet, simple things of life which are the real ones after all.

—LAURA INGALLS WILDER

I have known many, liked a few, loved only one, I toast to you.

—ANONYMOUS

Laugh and the world laughs with you. Snore and you sleep alone.

—ANTHONY BURGESS

Ephesians 4:32

Be ye kind to one another.

Accept the things to which fate binds you, and love the people with whom fate brings you together, but do so with all your heart.

—MARCUS AURELIUS

May "for better or worse" be far better than worse.

—ANONYMOUS

From *Bring Me a Unicorn*
ANNE MORROW LINDBERGH

Don't wish me happiness—it's gotten beyond that somehow. Wish me courage and strength and a sense of humor—I will need them all...

May the saddest day of your future be no worse than the happiest day of your past.

—ANONYMOUS

Irish Toasts

Toasts, or "blessings" as they are sometimes called, are an integral part of Irish culture unlike anywhere else in the world. These time-tested toasts have been beloved by many people regardless of their heritage.

May the road rise up to meet you,
May the wind be ever at your back,
May the sun shine warm upon your face,
The rain fall soft upon your fields,
And until we meet again,
May God hold you in the hollow of his hand.

A health to you
A wealth to you
And the best that life can give to you
May fortune still be kind to you.
And happiness be true to you,
And life be long and good to you
Is the toast of all your friends to you.

May there be a generation of children on the children
of your children.

May you have warm words on a cold evening
A full moon on a dark night
May the roof above you never fall in
And the friends gathered below never fall out
May you never be in want
And always have a soft pillow for your head
May you be in heaven an hour before
The devil knows you're dead

May you look back on the past with as much pleasure
as you look toward the future.

May you be poor in misfortunes and rich in blessings
Slow to make enemies and quick to make friends
And may you know nothing but happiness from this
day forward

May your home always be too small to hold all of your
friends

May love and laughter
Light your days,
And warm your heart and home.
May good and faithful friends be yours,
Wherever you may roam.
May peace and plenty
Bless your world,
With joy that long endures.
May all life's passing seasons
Bring the best to you and yours.

CREDITS

〜

I GRATEFULLY ACKNOWLEDGE the following sources, which are included in this book. They are listed alphabetically by the author's last name. An exhaustive effort has been made to clear all reprint permissions for this book. If any required acknowledgments have been omitted, it is unintentional. Upon receiving notification, the publishers will be pleased to rectify any omission in future editions.

Robert Frost: "The Master Speed" from *The Poetry of Robert Frost* edited by Edward Connery Lathem. Copyright 1936 by Robert Frost, © 1964 by Lesley Frost Ballantine, © 1969 by Henry Holt and Company. Reprinted by permission of Henry Holt and Company, LLC.

Kahlil Gibran: From *The Prophet* by Kahlil Gibran, copyright 1923 by Kahlil Gibran and renewed 1951 by Administrators C. T. A. of Kahlil Gibran Estate and Mary G. Gibran. Used by permission of Alfred A. Knopf, a division of Random House, Inc.

Ogden Nash: "A Word to Husbands" and "I Do, I Will, I Have" by Ogden Nash. Copyright © 1962, 1948 by Ogden Nash. Reprinted by permission of Curtis Brown, Ltd.

2:III:

ACKNOWLEDGMENTS

WITH GLASS IN HAND, I'd like to borrow some words from the well-known and propose toasts of gratitude to the following people.

Stewart, Tabori & Chang publisher Leslie Stoker: Despite Molière's claim that "Books and marriage go ill together," I am hopeful we shall prove otherwise!

Editor Beth Huseman: As the writer Walter Kerr once said of one of his colleagues, so I say of you—you "seemed less an editor of any sort than the very best sort of guardian angel." Good luck in your next realm of heaven.

The Studio Blue team: In the words of Raymond Loewy, "Good design keeps the user happy, the manufacturer in the black, and the aesthete unoffended." And, in this case, the author is appreciative.

Ann, Kathy & Adrian: Quoth the Bard, "Twixt such friends as we, few words suffice." Well, that is until Alan and I have the last word with toasts to you.

My husband and daughter: Thomas Jefferson sums up my sentiments exactly by saying, "It is in the love of one's family only that heartfelt happiness is known."

Cheers to you all.

INDEX